Hello, Family Members,

Learning to read is one of the most important accomplishments of early childhood. **Hello Reader!** books are designed to help children become skilled readers who like to read. Beginning readers learn to read by remembering frequently used words like "the," "is," and "and"; by using phonics skills to decode new words; and by interpreting picture and text clues. These books provide both the stories children enjoy and the structure they need to read fluently and independently. Here are suggestions for helping your child *before, during,* and *after* reading:

Before

- Look at the cover and pictures and have your child predict what the story is about.
- Read the story to your child.
- Encourage your child to chime in with familiar words and phrases.
- Echo read with your child by reading a line first and having your child read it after you do.

During

- Have your child think about a word he or she does not recognize right away. Provide hints such as "Let's see if we know the sounds" and "Have we read other words like this one?"
- Encourage your child to use phonics skills to sound out new words.
- Provide the word for your child when more assistance is needed so that he or she does not struggle and the experience of reading with you is a positive one.
- Encourage your child to have fun by reading with a lot of expression . . . like an actor!

After

- Have your child keep lists of interesting and favorite words.
- Encourage your child to read the books over and over again. Have him or her read to brothers, sisters, grandparents, and even teddy bears. Repeated readings develop confidence in young readers.
- Talk about the stories. Ask and answer questions. Share ideas about the funniest and most interesting characters and events in the stories.

I do hope that you and your child enjoy this book.

—Francie Alexander
Reading Specialist,
Scholastic's Instructional Publishing Group

For Adam, Elliot, and Nina
— F. R.

To Nathaniel
— J. D. Z.

Text copyright © 1999 by Fay Robinson.
Illustrations copyright © 1999 by Jean Day Zallinger.
All rights reserved. Published by Scholastic Inc.
SCHOLASTIC, HELLO READER! and CARTWHEEL BOOKS and associated logos are trademarks and/or registered trademarks of Scholastic Inc.

Library of Congress Cataloging-in-Publication Data
Robinson, Fay.
    Amazing lizards!/ by Fay Robinson; illustrated by Jean Day Zallinger.
        p.   cm.—(Hello reader! Science. Level 2)
    "Cartwheel books."
    Summary: Rhyming text and illustrations introduce the colorful world of lizards. Includes a reference section providing the names of the lizards.
    ISBN 0-590-33073-X
    1. Lizards — Juvenile literature. [1. Lizards.] I. Zallinger, Jean, ill. II. Title. III. Series.
QL666.L2R585 1999
597.95 — dc21   98-9171
                                                   CIP
                                                       AC

10 9 8 7 6 5 4 3   9/9 0/0 01 02 03 04

Printed in the U.S.A.   24
First printing, April 1999

Amazing LIZARDS!

by Fay Robinson
Illustrated by Jean Day Zallinger

Hello Reader ! Science — Level 2

SCHOLASTIC INC.
New York Toronto London Auckland Sydney

Plain old lizards, gray and green.

Lizards that you've never seen!

Amazing lizards splashed
with spots.

Yellow rings

and polka dots.

Bands and stripes

and long white lines.

Lizard skins with cool designs!

Lizards looking pretty weird…
wearing helmets.

Prickly beards.

Frilly collars,

beady scales.

Rhino horns and curly tails.

Lizards peering all around.

Lizards standing upside down.

Lizards line the rocky shores.
Don't they look like dinosaurs?

Lizards chomping lizard lunches —
moths and crickets,

eggs in bunches,

juicy cactus,

leaves and twigs...

Dragon lizards munching pigs!

Long, long tongues
for zapping flies.

Little tongues for lapping eyes.

Lively lizards taking swims.

Crossing rivers on two limbs.

Doing push-ups.

Racing by.

Lizards soaring through the sky.

Lizards flew by in a flash.

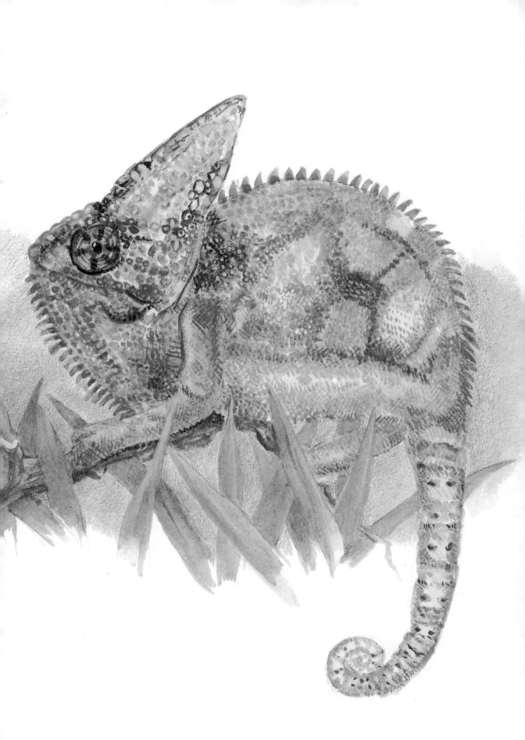

But we've saved the best for last!

Cover:
Jackson Chameleon

Page 5:
Carpet Chameleon

Page 8:
Lace Monitor

Page 8:
Trinidad Day Gecko

Page 3:
Tokay Gecko

Page 6:
Mauritius Day Gecko

Page 9:
Panther Chameleon

Page 4:
Whiptail

Page 7:
Timor Monitor

Page 7:
Tokay Gecko

Page 10:
Helmeted Lizard

Page 11:
Bearded Dragon

Page 14:
Meller's Chameleon

Page 17:
Six-Lined Race Runner

Page 12:
Frilled Lizard

Page 15:
House Gecko

Page 18:
Common Tegu

Page 18:
Land Iguana

Page 13:
Gila Monster

Page 13:
Jackson Chameleon

Page 16:
Marine Iguanas

Page 19:
Common Iguana

Pages 20-21:
Komodo Dragon

Page 22:
Meller's Chameleon

Page 22:
Leopard Lizard

Page 23:
Nile Monitors

Page 24:
Basilisk

Page 25:
Green Anole

Page 25:
Greater Earless Lizard

Page 26:
Toad-Headed Agama

Page 27:
Flying Dragons

Pages 28-29:
Veiled Chameleons